RIGHTS
NOW
EQUAL
OPPORTUNITY
ALL MEN
CREATED
EQUAL
BIRMINGHAM
MERCHANTS
UNFAIR

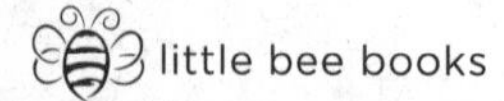

An imprint of Bonnier Publishing USA
251 Park Avenue South, New York, NY 10010

Manufactured in the United States LB 0917

Library of Congress Cataloging-in-Publication Data
Names: Ohlin, Nancy, author. | Simó, Roger, illustrator.
Title: Civil Rights Movement / by Nancy Ohlin; illustrated by Roger Simó.
Description: First edition. | New York, NY: Little Bee Books, [2017]
Series: Blast Back! | Includes bibliographical references and index.
Audience: Ages 7–10. | Subjects: LCSH: African Americans—Civil rights—History—Juvenile literature. | Civil rights movements—United States—History—20th century—Juvenile literature. | United States—Race relations—Juvenile literature.
Classification: LCC E185.61.O35 2017 | DDC 323.1196/073—dc23
LC record available at https://lccn.loc.gov/2017023557

Identifiers: LCCN 2017023557
ISBN 978-1-4998-0454-6 (pbk)
First Edition 10 9 8 7 6 5 4 3 2 1
ISBN 978-1-4998-0455-3 (hc)
First Edition 10 9 8 7 6 5 4 3 2 1

littlebeebooks.com
bonnierpublishingusa.com

THE CIVIL RIGHTS MOVEMENT

by Nancy Ohlin illustrated by Roger Simó

little bee books

OUT OF THE MOUNTAIN OF DESPAIR,
A STONE OF HOPE

CONTENTS

9 Introduction
12 A Brief History of the Civil Rights Movement
20 Slavery in America
26 Reconstruction
30 The Ku Klux Klan
40 Jim Crow Segregation
46 The Beginnings of the Civil Rights Movement
54 *Brown v. Board of Education*
61 Montgomery Bus Boycott
66 Martin Luther King Jr.
70 The Birmingham Demonstrations
76 March on Washington
84 New Civil Rights Laws
90 More Rioting and Violence
102 The Legacy of the Civil Rights Movement
110 Selected Bibliography

IT SEEMED LIKE REACHING FOR THE MOON
BARBARA JOHNS

Introduction

Have you ever heard people mention the civil rights movement and wondered what they were talking about? What are civil rights? Who was involved in the movement, and what were they fighting for?

Let's blast back in time for a little adventure and find out. . . .

OUT OF THE MOUNTAIN OF DESPAIR,
A STONE OF HOPE

A Brief History of the Civil Rights Movement

Civil rights are an individual's legally protected rights to social, political, economic, educational, and other similar opportunities. These rights must be the same for everyone regardless of individual characteristics such as race, religious beliefs, and national origin.

Black people in the United States have been deprived of their full civil rights since the time of slavery. The organized struggle for these civil rights, especially during the 1950s and 1960s, is called the civil rights movement. This movement resulted in many changes to the laws. It was also filled with much resistance—at times violent—from white people, including police officers and politicians.

The word "movement" refers to a group working together for a common cause. The word "civil" comes from the Latin word *civis*, which means "citizen." Some civil rights, such as the right to vote in elections, apply specifically to the citizens of a particular country. But other civil rights, such as the right to free speech, apply to all people who are living in or visiting that country, regardless of citizenship.

WE SHALL OVERCOME
FREE SPEECH

Civil Rights for All

The term "civil rights movement" is commonly used to describe the struggle for Black Americans to achieve equality. But other groups have had to fight—and continue to fight—for their civil rights, too. These groups include (but are not limited to)

Girls and women

Asian Americans

Muslim Americans

Hispanic Americans and Latino Americans

The LGBTQ (lesbian, gay, bisexual, transgender, and queer and/or questioning) community

People with disabilities

Senior citizens

Minority groups around the world

Human Rights

Human rights are the rights all people around the world are entitled to. They are not the same thing as civil rights, although the two can sometimes overlap.

In 1948, the United Nations—a multi-governmental organization that seeks to promote global peace, security, and cooperation—adopted the Universal Declaration of Human Rights (UDHR). The UDHR lists a number of human rights, including the right to live, be free, work, own property, marry, and have a family. The UDHR also lists prohibitions against things such as torture, inhuman punishment, and arbitrary arrest (which means being arrested without any reason or due process). The UDHR is not a code of law, however, but more of an aspirational document that spells out important principles and goals for the global community.

Slavery in America

Beginning around the year 1500, millions of Africans were forced to leave their homes and were brought to the Americas (aka "the New World"), to become slaves for the European colonists who lived there.

Under slavery, Africans were considered to be the "property" of their white "owners." They had to do whatever their owners wanted, including hard labor under horrific conditions. They were often beaten and abused. They had no freedom or rights.

Until 1865, some states in the United States were "slave states," which meant that slavery was legal within them. Others were "free states," which meant that slavery was illegal or being phased out of those territories.

The American Civil War took place between 1861 and 1865, largely over the issue of slavery. The anti-slavery Union (states and other lands that were mostly in the north) eventually defeated the pro-slavery Confederacy (states and other lands that were mostly in the south). This led to the end of slavery in the country.

The Emancipation Proclamation

On September 22, 1862, in the middle of the Civil War, President Abraham Lincoln issued a document that has come to be known as the Emancipation Proclamation. In it, President Lincoln declared that as of the first day of the new year, all enslaved people would be "thenceforth and forever free."

Of course, he could not enforce the proclamation in the states that were under the control of the South. Still, the document was important because (1) it affirmed the Civil War about slavery; and (2) it paved the way for freedmen (former slaves) to join the U.S. Army. Around 180,000 freedmen did join the army and helped to bring about the surrender of the South in 1865.

Reconstruction

The period after the Civil War was called Reconstruction and lasted until 1877. The idea was to "reconstruct" the nation and figure out how to go forward and set right the wrongs and inequities of slavery.

During Reconstruction, three amendments—the Thirteenth, Fourteenth, and Fifteenth—were added to the U.S. Constitution, granting freedmen and other Black people basic civil rights. (The Constitution is the document that spells out the fundamental laws and principles the country is governed by.) These amendments are sometimes referred to as the "Reconstruction Amendments."

The Thirteenth Amendment abolished slavery (and all involuntary servitude, which means being a servant against one's will). An exception was made if the involuntary servitude was meant to be a punishment for a crime.

The Fourteenth Amendment granted citizenship to anyone born or naturalized in the U.S. and provided equal protection under the laws for all citizens. (Naturalization is a process by which a foreign-born person can become a citizen.)

The Fifteenth Amendment said that U.S. citizens could not be denied the right to vote based on race, color, or past enslavement.

Unfortunately, these and other Reconstruction efforts did not end unfair treatment of (or violence against) Black people in America.

The Ku Klux Klan

The Ku Klux Klan (or KKK) is a hate organization that started right after the Civil War in 1866. Klan members believed in a doctrine of "white supremacy," which held that white people were superior to Black people and other non-white racial groups. They used violence, intimidation, and other terrorist tactics to try to keep freedmen from living in peace and exercising their newly granted civil rights (such as the right to vote).

The Ku Klux Klan (which comes in part from the Greek word *kyklos*, meaning "circle") was originally a social club of Confederate war veterans in Tennessee. Its leader was given the title of "grand wizard."

Klansmen wore white robes and hoods to hide their identities and to cause fear. They went on raids at night, beating and killing former slaves and their families and burning down their homes. They murdered Black politicians and other Black leaders. They also targeted white supporters of freedmen.

The first Ku Klux Klan organization lasted until the late 1870s. A second wave of the Klan started up in 1915 and expanded its circle of targets to include Jews, Catholics, immigrants, and other groups. Its membership reached four million in the 1920s.

These new Klansmen would sometimes leave a burning cross (the Klan's symbol) at the scene of their violent crimes.

The Ku Klux Klan still exists to this day, although in much smaller numbers and in separate, less-organized groups.

The Enforcement Acts

Congress passed the Enforcement Acts between 1870 and 1871. They were a set of laws that sought to protect the rights of Black people to vote, serve on juries, hold political office, and more. The main reason for the Enforcement Acts was to try to stop the Ku Klux Klan's reign of terror.

Before the Enforcement Acts, many states were reluctant to stand up to the Klan. Some were too weak or too afraid. Some state and local political leaders were even Klan members or sympathizers.

The Enforcement Acts allowed the federal government to step in if and when the states failed to protect its Black citizens. With the Enforcement Acts, President Ulysses S. Grant was able to send federal troops to the worst-hit areas to try to stop Klan violence.

WHITE
FARMERS CAFE

The Civil Rights Act of 1875

In 1875, Congress passed a civil rights act that was intended to guarantee an individual's access to various public facilities (such as inns and theaters), regardless of race or past enslavement. The new law also covered access to public transportation and the ability to serve on a jury.

Unfortunately, the Civil Rights Act of 1875 was hardly ever enforced. And in 1883, the Supreme Court (the highest court in the land) declared it unconstitutional, saying that it was not in line with the Thirteenth and Fourteenth Amendments.

The Compromise of 1877

Reconstruction came to an end in 1877 after the election of President Rutherford B. Hayes, who was a Republican. (The Republicans were more supportive of the rights of Black people than the Democrats.)

The 1876 election between Hayes and his Democratic opponent, Samuel J. Tilden, was too close to call. It hinged on which candidate had won the twenty electoral votes from Florida, Louisiana, South Carolina, and Oregon. To secure the presidency, Hayes and other Republican leaders made a deal with Democratic leaders. If the Democrats

allowed Hayes to become president, Hayes would pull federal troops out of the South. These were the troops that had been protecting freedmen at the polls and elsewhere. Hayes would also let Democrats take over the governments of Florida, Louisiana, and South Carolina, which at the time were the only Republican-controlled governments in the South.

With this compromise, Hayes became president. The era of the federal government trying to protect the rights of Black people was over.

Jim Crow Segregation

After the end of Reconstruction in 1877 and well into the twentieth century, some states, cities, and towns, mostly in the South, passed laws that perpetuated and enforced racial segregation (or separation). These laws are sometimes referred to as Jim Crow laws.

Jim Crow laws required that "people of color" (those with any Black ancestry) be separated from white people in public places such as inns, theaters, restaurants, parks, cemeteries, trains, and buses. Black children could not go to the same schools as white children. Jim Crow laws also kept Black men from voting. (Women did not have full voting rights until the Nineteenth Amendment to the Constitution in 1920.)

Who Was Jim Crow?

The use of "Jim Crow" as a racially charged term comes from a blackface minstrel routine called "Jump Jim Crow." Blackface minstrel shows consisted of song, dance, and theater routines performed by white actors wearing dark makeup so they could pretend to be Black. The idea was to mock Black people and perpetuate insulting racial stereotypes for the purpose of entertainment. A stereotype is a preconceived, incorrect idea—usually negative, and usually about a group of people—for example, "girls aren't good at sports" or "all Muslims are terrorists."

The Jump Jim Crow routine was created around 1828 by a white American actor named Thomas Dartmouth Rice. It was full of negative stereotypes about Black people. It was also extremely popular and created a demand for more minstrel shows in the U.S. and in England.

As a result of Jump Jim Crow, "Jim Crow" became a racist epithet (or term of abuse) and a term that highlighted the grim reality of segregation (as in Jim Crow laws).

Plessy v. Ferguson

In 1890, the state of Louisiana passed a Jim Crow law that said that passenger railway companies had to provide separate carriages (or cars) for white and Black people. The consequence of the law was that Black people could be arrested for sitting in the "all-white" carriage, and vice versa.

In 1892, a passenger named Homer Plessy, who was seven-eighths white and one-eighth Black, was arrested for sitting in a carriage that had been designated "all white." The case went all the way up to the Supreme Court. In 1896, the Supreme Court ruled that the Louisiana law was constitutional. The court's decision essentially allowed and perpetuated a "separate but equal" policy that kept Black Americans from sharing the same public facilities as white Americans.

The Beginnings of the Civil Rights Movement

Even though Black people tried to resist racism and segregation, it wasn't until the twentieth century that an organized movement for change began.

One of the most important early leaders of the civil rights movement was named W. E. B. Du Bois. An American sociologist and professor, he felt that protests (public demonstrations of disapproval or disagreement) and civil disobedience (refusing to obey unjust laws) were necessary to achieve equality for Black people. One of his most famous books, *The Souls of Black Folk* (1903), encouraged Black people to fight for equality and not settle for anything less.

Du Bois helped found the National Association for the Advancement of Colored People (NAACP), an organization dedicated to ending race-based discrimination, in 1909. (Discrimination is the unfair treatment of a person or group of people based on such things as race, religion, or age.) White citizens

worked together with Black citizens within the NAACP because they wanted to end the race riots and other terrible events tied to racial struggles of the time. A race riot is a violent public disturbance over racial conflicts. Among other actions, the NAACP used—and continues to use—the courts to fight for civil rights.

Booker T. Washington

Booker Taliaferro Washington was an educator and Black leader whose views were often at odds with the views of W. E. B. Du Bois. Washington believed that compromise, hard work, and patience—not protest—were the keys to ending racism.

Born into slavery in 1856 in Virginia, he and his mother gained their freedom in 1865 and moved to West Virginia. Despite extreme poverty, he earned an education and went on to become a teacher. In 1881, he was chosen to head a new school for Black Americans in Alabama. By 1915, he had helped the school grow from a few students to approximately 1,500. Today, it is Tuskegee University.

Washington was the first Black person whose face appeared on a U.S. postage stamp and also a U.S. coin.

World War I and World War II

Black Americans served courageously in both world wars (and in other U.S. wars, too) despite discrimination and segregation in the military and elsewhere. Approximately 350,000 Black Americans served with the United States Armed Forces in World War I, and over a million Black Americans served in World War II. In 1948, President Harry S. Truman issued an executive order to end racial discrimination in the armed forces.

Brown v. Board of Education

The NAACP's most famous success in the courts is the case of *Brown v. Board of Education* (of Topeka, Kansas).

The NAACP's lawyers, led by Thurgood Marshall, argued before the nine justices that having separate schools for white and Black children was unconstitutional. The Supreme Court agreed. Their ruling was handed down on May 17, 1954, with a unanimous (9–0) vote. Marshall went on to become the first Black justice of the Supreme Court in 1967.

The *Brown v. Board of Education* case essentially nullified the *Plessy v. Ferguson* "separate but equal" case of 1896. It marked an important turning point in the struggle for civil rights.

However, achieving desegregation in schools would be an uphill battle for many decades to come.

The Little Rock Nine

There was a great deal of resistance to the *Brown v. Board of Education* decision, especially in the southern states. One of the most dramatic examples of this happened in Little Rock, Arkansas.

In the summer of 1957, nine Black students enrolled in the Little Rock Central High School, which had been all white until then.

When the nine students tried to walk into the school in September, they were met by a big mob of white protesters who blocked their way, yelled, threw stones, and threatened to kill them. In addition, the governor of Arkansas, Orval Eugene Faubus, sent approximately 280 soldiers from the Arkansas National Guard to prevent the nine students from entering the school. They went home but managed to enter the school through a side door several weeks later.

Protected by federal soldiers, the Little Rock Nine bravely continued attending the school, despite more verbal and physical attacks from their fellow students. The situation drew national and international attention to the racism still rampant in the U.S.

In 1958, one of the Little Rock Nine, Ernest Green, became the first Black student to graduate from the school. That same year, Governor Faubus was re-elected. He proceeded to close all the schools in Little Rock rather than submit to the federal government's orders to desegregate (or end segregation). Little Rock Central High finally reopened in 1960 with a desegregated student body.

Ruby Bridges

In 1960, six-year-old Ruby Bridges tried to walk into her new school, the Frantz Elementary School in New Orleans, which up until then had been all white. She was met by an angry white mob that yelled at her and threatened her. Escorted by her mother and federal marshals to protect her, she bravely continued attending the school. She became the first Black child to attend an all-white public elementary school in the South. As an adult, she went back to the Frantz School to help make it a better school.

Montgomery Bus Boycott

On December 1, 1955, in Montgomery, Alabama, a Black woman named Rosa Parks refused to give up her seat on a bus to a white man. She was arrested for violating one of the city's racial segregation laws.

On December 5, a group of Black people held a one-day boycott of the Montgomery public buses to protest Rosa Parks's arrest. They then decided to keep the bus boycott going and created the Montgomery Improvement Association (MIA). The MIA elected as their president a twenty-six-year-old local pastor named Martin Luther King Jr.

On November 13, 1956, the Supreme Court affirmed that Montgomery's segregated bus seating was unconstitutional. The city was ordered to integrate its bus system, and the boycott came to an end on December 20, after 381 days.

Rosa Parks

Rosa Louise McCauley was born in Tuskegee, Alabama, on February 4, 1913. She married Raymond Parks in 1932, and the two of them worked with the local NAACP chapter.

Her activism for the rights of Black people did not begin or end with her refusal to give up her seat on the bus in 1955. Activism means working and campaigning for social or political change. She worked tirelessly as an NAACP leader and in other capacities to try to expose injustices and end racism.

After the Montgomery bus boycott, she was fired from her job as a seamstress. She also received death threats. She and her family moved to Detroit, Michigan, in 1957. There, she worked for Congressman John Conyers from 1965 until she retired in 1988.

Parks received the Presidential Medal of Freedom in 1996 and the Congressional Gold Medal of Honor in 1999.

Martin Luther King Jr.

As a result of the Montgomery bus boycott, Dr. Martin Luther King Jr. became one of the most important leaders of the national civil rights movement.

Dr. King was born in Atlanta, Georgia, in 1929. After college, he spent three years at a seminary (a school for religious study). There, he learned about the concept of nonviolent resistance, such as boycotts. He believed that nonviolent protests were the best way to achieve equality for Black people.

Dr. King went on to earn a doctorate in theology. In 1954, he became the pastor of the Dexter Avenue Baptist Church in

Montgomery, Alabama. In 1957, he organized a group dedicated to peaceful civil rights activities. This group was called the Southern Christian Leadership Conference (SCLC), which still exists today.

In 1964, King was awarded the Nobel Peace Prize. In 1983, a law was passed to make Dr. King's birthday a national holiday.

Sit-Ins and Freedom Rides

In the early 1960s, activists began engaging in sit-ins and Freedom Rides to protest nonviolently.

With sit-ins, Black people would go to places where they would not be served—for example, a segregated restaurant—and sit down and refuse to leave. Even if they were harassed or arrested, they remained nonviolent. These sit-ins gained sympathy for the civil rights cause.

With Freedom Rides, white and Black people rode buses together throughout the South to make sure buses and bus stations were not segregated. Unfortunately, Freedom Riders were met by a lot of hostility and violence, including in Alabama, where a bus was bombed. Some Freedom Riders were also arrested. Still, the Freedom Rides drew national and international attention and resulted in changes to laws regarding segregation in interstate bus terminals.

The Birmingham Demonstrations

In the spring of 1963, Dr. Martin Luther King Jr. and other activists participated in mass demonstrations and other nonviolent protest activities in Birmingham, Alabama. On April 7, the public safety commissioner of the city, Eugene "Bull" Conner, ordered the police to sic attack dogs on the protesters. Dr. King and others were arrested.

RIGHTS
NOW
EQUAL
OPPORTUNITY
ALL MEN CREATED EQUAL
BIRMINGHAM MERCHANTS UNFAIR

While in prison, Dr. King penned the now-famous “Letter from Birmingham Jail.” In the letter, he explained why nonviolent protest was necessary to fight racism. “Injustice anywhere is a threat to justice everywhere,” he wrote.

On May 3, Birmingham police used high-pressure fire hoses against a group of peaceful demonstrators, mostly students. This drew national attention, and the situation in Birmingham led the federal government to step in and negotiate a settlement between the various factions, including Birmingham's city officials and white business owners.

But after a settlement was announced, more violence ensued as the KKK bombed the A. G. Gaston Motel, which Dr. King and his fellow activists had been using to organize the protests, as well as the home of Dr. King's younger brother, Reverend A. D. King.

March on Washington

In June of 1963, President John F. Kennedy—who was a supporter of civil rights—made a speech asking Congress to pass a new bill that would prohibit discrimination in public places, hiring for jobs, and government programs.

On August 28, 1963, an interracial group of more than 200,000 gathered in Washington, D.C., to urge the government to pass the bill. This event was called the "March on Washington" (short for the "March on Washington for Jobs and Freedom").

At the march, Dr. Martin Luther King Jr. gave his iconic "I Have a Dream" speech near the Lincoln Memorial. In his speech, he reminded everyone that the crafters of the U.S. Constitution and the Declaration of Independence had promised "life, liberty, and the pursuit of happiness" for

all Americans. "Now is the time to make real the promises of democracy," he said. "Now is the time to rise from the dark and desolate valley of segregation to the sunlit path of racial justice."

Unfortunately, the march did not convince Congress to pass the civil rights bill.

The 16th Street Baptist Church Bombing

A few weeks after the March on Washington, a bomb went off at the 16th Street Baptist Church in Birmingham, Alabama, killing four young girls and injuring several dozen others. The church, which had a mostly Black congregation, was also a meeting place for civil rights activists. Though four suspects were named in the crime, none of them would be brought to trial.

It was later revealed that the head of the Federal Bureau of Investigation (FBI), J. Edgar Hoover, had accumulated evidence against the bombers, but refused to share it with county prosecutors. Hoover did not approve of the civil rights movement. More than a decade after the attack, the case was reopened, and three Ku Klux Klan members were eventually brought to trial for the bombings, found guilty, and sent to prison. The fourth suspect died before he could be tried.

New Civil Rights Laws

After President Kennedy was assassinated in November of 1963, President Lyndon B. Johnson vowed to get the civil rights bill passed. He succeeded in June of 1964.

This law, known as the Civil Rights Act of 1964, is one of the most important pieces of legislation in US history. It outlawed any discrimination based on one's "race, color, religion, or national origin." (A previous civil rights bill had been passed in 1957, but it was not as strong or comprehensive as the 1964 one.)

However, Black people continued to face obstacles voting. Consequently, President Johnson called for a federal law to ensure equality at the polls. The result was the Voting Rights Act of 1965, which ended state and local laws that restricted voting rights and led to a greater increase in the number of Black voters.

Freedom Summer

In the summer of 1964, civil rights groups helped organize a voter registration project called the Mississippi Summer Project, or Freedom Summer. The project was part of a larger mission to increase Black voter registration in the South. The project was met by much resistance and violence, however, and resulted in the murder of three young registration workers by Klansmen.

The Selma to Montgomery March

In March of 1965, Dr. King and the SCLC helped organize a protest march from Selma, Alabama, to Montgomery (the capital of Alabama) for the cause of Black voter registration in the South. Under the protection of National Guard troops after two earlier efforts had failed, the protesters marched nonstop for three days to finally reach Montgomery. Events like this march and Freedom Summer helped push the passage of the Voting Rights Act of 1965.

EDMUND PETTUS BRIDGE

More Rioting and Violence

Despite the Civil Rights Act of 1964 and the Voting Rights Act of 1965, Black Americans continued to suffer from social and economic inequalities, especially in cities. Unemployment, poverty, discrimination, and other problems had not gone away.

Some people in the civil rights movement believed that amends needed to be made for the many injustices that the Black community had suffered in the past and that continued to plague them in the present, while others felt that nonviolent protest was not enough to achieve their goals.

There were more race riots and violence across the country between 1964 and 1968 as tensions ran high between white and Black citizens, and between Black citizens and the police. In 1964, hundreds of people rioted in the Harlem and Bedford-Stuyvesant neighborhoods of New York City when a white police officer shot a fifteen-year-old Black boy

named James Powell. In 1965, riots in the Watts and other predominantly Black neighborhoods of South-Central Los Angeles resulted in thirty-four deaths and over a thousand injured. Similar riots occurred in Detroit, Michigan; Newark, New Jersey; and across the country.

On April 4, 1968, Dr. King was assassinated by a sniper's bullet while standing on the balcony of a motel in Memphis, Tennessee. As a result, more riots erupted in over a hundred U.S. cities. A white man named James Earl Ray confessed to the murder the following year, then recanted, saying he had been forced to confess and was innocent of the crime.

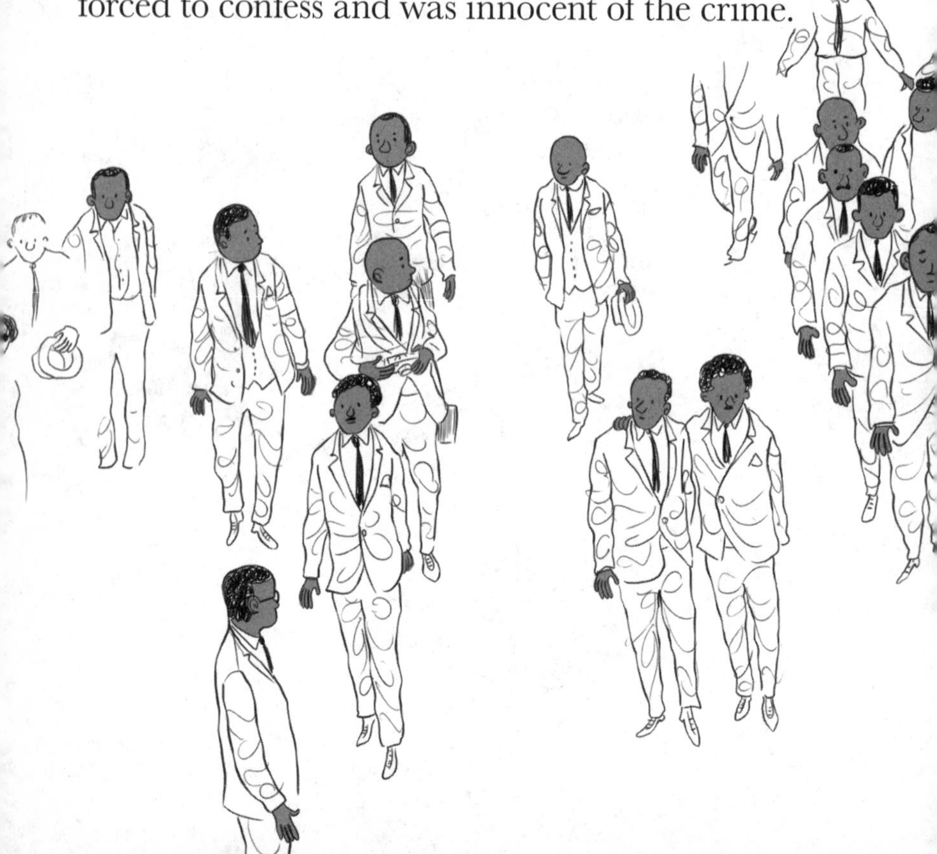

Some felt that Dr. King's death marked the end of the civil rights movement, while others felt that it marked the beginning of a new chapter in the struggle for equality.

The Black Power Movement

The Black Power movement of the 1960s and 1970s grew out of a fundamental disagreement with nonviolent protest as the answer to injustice, and also a call for Black pride. This movement had many different leaders, factions, and philosophies.

One influential faction was the Black Panther Party, which was founded in 1966 and sought to stop police brutality and other oppressive practices against Black people. Another influential faction

was the Nation of Islam, which disagreed with many of the goals of the civil rights movement and wanted to establish a separate nation for Black people.

Malcolm X was an important leader in the Nation of Islam. But in 1964, he left the group due to ideological and other differences and started the Organization of Afro-American Unity (OAAU). He converted to Sunni Islam; he also grew to believe that white people were victims of racism just as much as Black people. He advocated Pan-Africanism and encouraged all citizens of African descent to unify and form bonds.

He was assassinated on February 21, 1965, by three members of the Nation of Islam.

Women in the Civil Rights Movement

In addition to Rosa Parks and Ruby Bridges, many other women and girls played vital roles in the civil rights movement, and yet they remain relatively unknown compared to their male counterparts. Here are just a few:

Barbara Johns:
In 1951, at the age of sixteen, Johns led her fellow students in a protest to demand equal rights at their Virginia high school. Their protest became part of the *Brown v. Board of Education* case.

Claudette Colvin: Nine months before Rosa Parks refused to give up her seat on the bus in 1955, fifteen-year-old Colvin had done the same and was arrested. She helped end segregation on buses in Montgomery, Alabama.

Septima Poinsette Clark: As part of the SCLC, she was instrumental in setting up "citizenship schools" to promote Black voter registration.

Ella Baker: Formerly a director of the SCLC, she was one of the founders of the Student Nonviolent Coordinating Committee (SNCC) in 1960.

Fannie Lou Hamer: A tireless civil rights activist, she was one of the organizers of the Mississippi Freedom Summer for the SNCC.

Coretta Scott King: The widow of Dr. King, she founded the Martin Luther King Jr. Center for Nonviolent Change in Atlanta in 1968.

Myrlie Evers-Williams: The widow of slain civil rights activist Medgar Evers, she went on to become the first female head of the NAACP (in 1995).

The Legacy of the Civil Rights Movement

The decades following the Civil Rights Act of 1964 have brought more changes and progress in the struggle for equality. The civil rights movement also inspired and energized other civil rights movements.

Some civil rights leaders, including John Lewis and Jesse Jackson, went on to have distinguished careers in electoral politics. And in 2007, the United States elected its first Black president, Barack Obama, who was then re-elected for a second term.

Today, an important international organization called Black Lives Matter fights for Black civil rights, especially regarding racial profiling (which means suspecting a person of having committed a crime based on his or her race or ethnicity), police brutality against Black people, and other forms of racism. The NAACP, SCLC, the Committee on Racial Equality (CORE), and other groups continue to contribute to the cause.

Unfortunately, discrimination and violence are still part of American society, not just against Black people, but toward other groups, too. Muslim Americans are all-too-common targets, as well as members of the LGBTQ community and many others.

Hopefully, courageous activists and leaders will continue to work fiercely and passionately to fulfill the promise of life, liberty, and the pursuit of happiness for *all* Americans.

The National Museum of African American History

The National Museum of African American History and Culture opened in Washington, D.C., in September of 2016. Congress passed a law in 2003 to establish this museum as part of the Smithsonian Institution, so when it opened, it became the nineteenth Smithsonian museum. According to the museum's website, "it is the only national museum devoted exclusively to the documentation of African American life, history, and culture."

Well, it's been a great adventure. Goodbye, Civil Rights Movement!

Where to next?

Also available:

Selected Bibliography

Adams, Noah. "The Inspiring Force of 'We Shall Overcome.'" *NPR*. August 28, 2013. http://www.npr.org/2013/08/28/216482943/the-inspiring-force-of-we-shall-overcome.

Adler, Margot. "Before Rosa Parks, There Was Claudette Colvin." *NPR*. March 15, 2009. http://www.npr.org/templates/story/story.php?storyId=101719889.

"Birmingham Demonstrations." *Civil Rights Digital Library*. 2013. http://crdl.usg.edu/events/birmingham_demonstrations.

Britannica Kids. kids.britannica.com.

Encyclopedia Britannica. britannica.com.

King, Jr., Dr. Martin Luther. "Letter from Birmingham Jail." April 16, 1963. http://kingencyclopedia.stanford.edu/kingweb/popular_requests/frequentdocs/birmingham.pdf.

McBride, Alex. "Landmark Cases: *Plessy v. Ferguson*." *PBS*. 2007. http://www.pbs.org/wnet/supremecourt/antebellum/landmark_plessy.html.

"The Rise and Fall of Jim Crow." *PBS*. 2002. http://www.pbs.org/wnet/jimcrow.

"Selma to Montgomery March." *History*. 2010. http://www.history.com/topics/black-history/selma-montgomery-march.

"Universal Declaration of Human Rights." *United Nations*. December 10, 1948. http://www.un.org/en/universal-declaration-human-rights.

Walling, William English. "The Race War in the North." *Independent*. September 1, 1908. http://www.eiu.edu/past_tracker/AfricanAmerican_Independent65_3Sept1908_RaceWarInTheNorth.pdf.

"Women Had Key Roles in Civil Rights Movement." *NBC News*. October 29, 2005. http://www.nbcnews.com/id/9862643/ns/us_news-life/t/women-had-key-roles-civil-rights-movement/#.WIeWUbYrKRs.

NANCY OHLIN is the author of the YA novels *Always, Forever* and *Beauty* as well as the early chapter book series Greetings from Somewhere under the pseudonym Harper Paris. She lives in Ithaca, New York, with her husband, their two kids, four cats, and assorted animals who happen to show up at their door. Visit her online at nancyohlin.com.

ROGER SIMÓ is an illustrator based in a town near Barcelona, where he lives with his wife, son, and daughter. He has become the person that he would have envied when he was a child: someone who makes a living by drawing and explaining fantastic stories.